# The Farmer in the Dell

The
Child's
World®

Distributed by The Child's World®
1980 Lookout Drive • Mankato, MN 56003-1705
800-599-READ • www.childsworld.com

Acknowledgments
The Child's World®: Mary Berendes, Publishing Director
The Design Lab: Kathleen Petelinsek, Design

Library of Congress Cataloging-in-Publication Data
Ferraro Close, Laura.
The farmer in the dell / illustrated by Laura Ferraro Close.
    p. cm.
ISBN 978-1-60954-296-2 (library bound: alk. paper)
1. Folk songs, English—United States—Texts. [1. Folk songs—United States.
2. Singing games. 3. Games.] I. Title.
PZ8.3.F3685Far 2011
782.42—dc22
[E]                              2010032423

Printed in the United States of America in Mankato, Minnesota.
December 2010
PA02074

**ILLUSTRATED BY LAURA FERRARO CLOSE**

The farmer in the dell,
the farmer in the dell.
Hi-ho, the derry-o,
the farmer in the dell.

The farmer takes his wife,
the farmer takes his wife.
Hi-ho, the derry-o,
the farmer takes his wife.

The wife takes their child,
the wife takes their child.
Hi-ho, the derry-o,
the wife takes their child.

The child takes a nurse,
the child takes a nurse.
Hi-ho, the derry-o,
the child takes a nurse.

The nurse takes a dog,
the nurse takes a dog.
Hi-ho, the derry-o,
the nurse takes a dog.

The dog takes a cat,
the dog takes a cat.
Hi-ho, the derry-o,
the dog takes a cat.

The cat takes a rat,
the cat takes a rat.
Hi-ho, the derry-o,
the cat takes a rat.

The rat takes the cheese,
the rat takes the cheese.
Hi-ho, the derry-o,
the rat takes the cheese.

The cheese stands alone,
the cheese stands alone.

Hi-ho, the derry-o,
the cheese stands alone.

# SONG ACTIVITY

The farmer in the dell,
the farmer in the dell.
Hi-ho, the derry-o,
the farmer in the dell.

The farmer takes his wife,
the farmer takes his wife.
Hi-ho, the derry-o,
the farmer takes his wife.

The wife takes their child,
the wife takes their child.
Hi-ho, the derry-o,
the wife takes their child.

The child takes a nurse,
the child takes a nurse.
Hi-ho, the derry-o,
the child takes a nurse.

The nurse takes a dog,
the nurse takes a dog.
Hi-ho, the derry-o,
the nurse takes a dog.

The dog takes a cat,
the dog takes a cat.
Hi-ho, the derry-o,
the dog takes a cat.

The cat takes a rat,
the cat takes a rat.
Hi-ho, the derry-o,
the cat takes a rat.

The rat takes the cheese,
the rat takes the cheese.
Hi-ho, the derry-o,
the rat takes the cheese.

The cheese stands alone,
the cheese stands alone.
Hi-ho, the derry-o,
the cheese stands alone.

Players join hands and make a circle around one player. This player is the "farmer." The circle moves around the farmer until the verse ends and it's time for the farmer to "choose" (a wife, a child, etc.). The farmer chooses someone in the outer circle to be the wife (child, etc.), and he or she joins the farmer in the center. On the last verse, the player picked as the "cheese" stands alone in the middle, and the rest of the players return to the outer circle. The "cheese" player becomes the "farmer" for the next game.

# BENEFITS OF NURSERY RHYMES AND ACTIVITY SONGS

**Activity songs and nursery rhymes are more than just a fun way to pass the time. They are a rich source of intellectual, emotional, and physical development for a young child. Here are some of their benefits:**

❁ Learning the words and activities builds the child's self-confidence—"I can do it all by myself!"

❁ The repetitious movements build coordination and motor skills.

❁ The close physical interaction between adult and child reinforces both physical and emotional bonding.

❁ In a context of "fun," the child learns the art of listening in order to learn.

❁ Learning the words expands the child's vocabulary. He or she learns the names of objects and actions that are both familiar and new.

❁ Repeating the words helps develop the child's memory.

❁ Learning the words is an important step toward learning to read.

❁ Reciting the words gives the child a grasp of English grammar and how it works. This enhances the development of language skills.

❁ The rhythms and rhyming patterns sharpen listening skills and teach the child how poetry works. Eventually the child learns to put together his or her own simple rhyming words— "I made a poem!"

# ABOUT THE ILLUSTRATOR

Laura Ferraro Close got her start as an illustrator twenty-five years ago, working as a greeting card artist for a card company in Kansas City, Missouri. Today, Laura lives near Boston with her husband, two sons, a sweet dog, and two guinea pigs.